GOLDEN STEPS & 5A'S TO SUCCESS

Rajesh H. Kulkarni /

Sumesh G. Menon

Uma Publications Nanded

ISBN: 978-81-937011-8-8 (paperback)
Golden Steps & 5A's to Success

Publisher: Himanshu Kulkarni,
Uma Publications
C/O R.B.Karkare, Karkare Niwas,
Mill Road, Kalamandir, Nanded.
Cell: 9421850831
Mail: umapublicationsned@gmail.com,
Website: www.umapublishinghouse.com

Manuscript Review: Dr. Gowri Menon
Cover Design: Sriram Kulkarni
Cell: 9975477661
Layout: Ms.Swati Karkare
Drawings and Images: Nidhi Rahul Kulkarni

Printed by: Amazon KDP
Edition: 2020 Vol-1

Price Rs.120/-

DEDICATION

To
My siblings (Rahul, Pallavi, Himanshu) for their untiring assistance and endearing encouragement.

To my parents (Sow.Uma and Shri. H.R. Kulkarni) for showing utmost patience during my turbulent adolescence and who have been a great source of inspiration for authoring this book.

My wife (Vidya) for bringing normalcy to this rocking boat and being my strong support system

My Daughter (Phani) for being a true fighter and my fiercest shield.

My friends, without whom my journey would have been less meaningful.

Rajesh H. Kulkarni

To
My father Late Shri. N.M. Gopinath Menon for passing on the legacy of empathy, ideology, care, compassion, respect and love. I owe my present day success to him and the values I have learnt from him.

All my Family members - my mother (Mrs.Saraswathi Menon), my elder Brothers and Family (Mr.Suresh Menon and Family, Mr.Sudhish Menon and Family) for all their encouragement till date. They were a great source of motivation when I started out on my journey.

My Wife (Gowri Menon) for the enthusiasm shown throughout my penning of this book, and always being there for me; and my dear son (Sujal Menon) for playing the role of stimulant while I was writing this book:)

Last but never the least, I wish to dedicate this book to all my school and college friends, as well as all my (ex) colleagues till date for their unending motivation and staunch moral support.

Sumesh G. Menon

PREFACE

At the outset, let us give you a brief about our authors, and the reasons why they set out to write this incredibly useful book!

Authors are Rajesh H. Kulkarni and Sumesh G. Menon.

Sumesh Menon has more than 25 years of experience in the IT industry, associated with various roles and having handled several complex responsibilities. He has worked largely with multinational companies and is currently employed as Chief Strategy Officer of a software company based out of Pune.

He is an excellent leader with entrepreneurship skills, who believes in team work and effectively manages teams across geographies, business horizontals and verticals.

He is a process oriented person with expertise in consulting, global delivery management and strategy creation. He has successfully managed large and complex programs for several global organisations.

He has dynamically worked with different cultures and gained expertise in building high performance teams.

He has also had a small stint of running his own venture for some time , so as to understand first-hand, the pain areas of being an entrepreneur.

He holds an MBA in Consultancy management from Bits Pilani, and is an engineer in the Electronics and Telecom discipline from Marathwada University.

In his free time, he enjoys socialising with friends. He also loves devoting time to visit institutes and guide students, and coach and mentor budding entrepreneurs. He is very passionate about playing table-tennis and badminton. He also likes to explore new places and spend quality time with family and friends. He is curious about cooking and tries new recipes. He is very fond of singing.

Rajesh has around 24+ years of experience in academics in Education sector. Dr. Rajesh Kulkarni is Director of Smt Indira Gandhi College of Engineering, Ghansoli, Navi Mumbai. He is also Constant Mentor at Ignition Incubation Center and a passionate teacher, motivating speaker, author, publisher and a change agent for organizational transformation.

His Webinars/Seminars/FDPs reached more than 15000 participants who got immensely benefitted. He is Founder of Uma Publications Nanded.

He is a Distant Associate for IP Adventure LLP Company an

IPR start-up. He published five books, many research papers and eight patents.

The authors have been friends since childhood, besides having studied together from Grade 2 right up to Under-graduation.

They parted ways to pursue education in their chosen fields, and then went on to make glorious careers. They met after 15 years and got connected quickly because of the old friendship.

Rajesh as a Professor and Director has interacted with thousands of students till date and also interacted with hundreds of researchers, faculties, Industry people, colleagues, juniors and seniors.

Similarly, Sumesh has had the good fortune to interact with thousands of employees from various companies and countries; ranging from Campus hires, freshers of 0 to 2 years to people with rich experience of 3 to 55 years; and who have handled various roles ranging from Software Developers to the CEO level.

Book Introduction

While discussing their journey over the past several years, they realized that they had garnered vast experience in their chosen paths, and that sharing such tremendous experience in their respective fields, the host of challenges they were privy to, and the success gained out the level of interactions they had with various functional heads, were indeed definitely immense learnings for the new generation of students just embarking on their career path.

They instantly felt the need to bring their experience to the table, so that it helps students and members across the industry from education to software in such a way that it helps people succeed in their career and enable them avoid those mistakes often unintentionally committed during their initial working tenure.

This book is made up of 2 sections

1. The Golden Steps to Succeed in Career
2. 5A's for Success and Growth

Rajesh has contributed towards the first section of the book, "The Golden Steps to Succeed in a Career" keeping in mind his years of experience amidst graduating students.

Sumesh, on the other hand, was interested to share the "5 A's for Success and Growth" in a career keeping in mind the employees in the companies he has interacted with throughout his career - from freshers, to the most significant position of CEO of the company –and based on his experience and interaction with, learning from and observation of various colleagues.

They believe that if this book is read by a family, it should definitely help them, since a family has a high probability of housing either a student or a job-seeking adult or one who is already in a job but faces challenges; and this book will be able to provide them the required tips to be successful.

As they are concluding this book during the COVID Period, they deemed it humane that 20% of the profits generated in the sale of this book will be donated for Purchasing PPE kits or helping the poor with essential goods. So, in effect, each person purchasing this book, would also be contributing indirectly to this noble initiative.

Acknowledgements

We render our gratitude to Mr. Shriram Kulkarni for the elegant Cover art of this book.

Dr. Gowri Menon patiently reviewed our manuscript multiple times and improvised the book and brought it to readable shape. We appreciate the same wholeheartedly.

Young Nidhi Kulkarni designed all the images of the book.

We are also thankful to Mr. Sunil Jadhav- Trustee JNISTR Institutes, Mr. Rajesh Apte- Founder Readitorium, Ms. Srishti Arora and Mr. Piyush Kumar- Cofounders Agriforetell, for their inputs during our research. It provided the much needed insights to complete this book.

We are also thankful to Mr. Sankul Rathod, Ms. Priyanka Shirsat and Mr. Vaibhav Thorat who are students of Dr. Rajesh Kulkarni and presently pursuing their higher studies in Germany and Ireland. Inputs from them have added perspective to the content laid out in this book.

Rajesh H. Kulkarni
Sumesh G. Menon

Table of Contents

Part – 1

Golden Steps to Success

1

SELECTING AN ENGINEERING COLLEGE

11th and 12th meaning Higher Secondary Education are the two critical years in the life of a student. They decide the future career path. These two years are the most stressful for the entire family. Sacrifices, adjustments, expenses and fear of the future are common characteristics during these times. Once all exams including MHCET and JEE are completed the core team of family members and the student relax a bit. This actually is the most crucial time and the team has to be on their toes and do their homework properly. The first thing the student and his family should do is identify a list of probable colleges where the student may get admission. Post that they should personally visit the college, meet principal, deans, heads of departments staff and students. During their visits to colleges ask the following critical questions:

- PhD-awarded senior Professors per department, their research publications in standard journals like Scopus/ web of sciences, research funding sanctioned to them from government, and patents published
- State of the art laboratories: Are the labs gearing up for Industry 4.0 and Industry 5.0? Computing power capable of handling big data / cloud / data analytics / machine learning / artificial intelligence / block chain / RPA projects and practical for computer engineering. For Civil engineering students' simulation software like tekla, staad, ETABS, BIM and primavera are being used in the labs. Do electrical and electronics engineering branches have labs catering to cyberphiscal systems in the form of embedded systems and IOT (Internet of Things)? Do they have PLC automation labs, simulation software for power system and circuit design?
- Start-up Incubation Centre: Is there a fully functional Start-up incubation centre eco-system.
- Industry- Academia Collaboration: Do they have industry sponsored labs and courses designed specifically as per industry requirements?
- Advanced Labs: Robotics, Mechatronics, 3D Printing labs which offers hands on learning training courses
- Do they have an active Training and Placement Cell with training schedules executed successfully and top companies like google / TCS / Accenture and branch wise core companies visited the college for placement drives?

Student clubs, support for competitive examinations and higher education opportunities are also desired nowadays. To sum it all does the college have an ecosystem to nurture the dream of a student in to reality.

Most important of all do they have a Covid-free environment and technology tools for course content delivery online? Can most of the activities like admission, exam form, fees, bonafides and recommendation letters be online?

2

SUCCESS MANTRA FOR ENGINEERING STUDENTS

Industry Expectations from Engineering Students

A good job in a well-rated MNC company is what a parent desires, when he admits his ward in an engineering college. A millennial these days aspires to take up a job with the desire that his salary will cater for an independent upscale lifestyle. An industry absorbs a fresher with a few minimal expectations.

The first and foremost expectation is can the candidate speak, think and gradually become a problem solver. The two primary expectations from a fresh engineering graduate is technology updating and good communication skills. One should have at least one area of expertise where he/she can show confidence. He should have desire and hunger to grow. His articulation of thoughts should be proper. He must have need for achievements, autonomy, risk taking ability, drive and determination, belief in himself. The other characteristics expected are flexibility, team spirit, learnability, zeal, positive attitude, self-motivation, adaptability and consistency. One should be skilled to speak multiple languages and if possible at least one foreign language. Awareness of current market trends can be an icing on the cake.

All the above skillsets can be acquired through practice and determination. To learn any of the above skillsets there are two ways; participation in college activities, events, contests, internships and online resources. Collection of artefacts in the form of certificates of achievements and making them visible in the resume during interview will enhance chances of getting selected.

The most important aspect of preparation for the interview by a fresher is the final year project. The candidate should be able to explain the purpose of the project, outcomes and the contribution with conviction. It should be capable of defining one's roadmap for growth.

3

HIGHER EDUCATION IN FOREIGN UNIVERSITIES

Higher Education in Germany

Most of the public funded Universities do not charge any fees, as education is free. After joining the University students have to pay student association fee of around 100 Euros which takes care of semester passes for commuting and few other services like hostel support. When you apply to German Universities, one of the mandatory clauses is that you have to block funds to the tune of 8-9 lakhs INR per year in a German registered bank and every month, the student gets between 800-900 Euros from the blocked amount. This figure is derived by the Government as approximate expenses per month which may be incurred. The total cost for a Master's program is estimated to be around 15 lakh INR which may vary depending on living standards of a person. Though education is free for public funded universities, private universities charge a fee. The good news for Ph.D. aspirants is that Germany as per experts is a very good option for Ph.D. as Scholars get their degree within three years because of meticulous planning and scheduling. Further, 3000 Euros stipend is paid to students pursuing Ph.D. What's more, Schengen VISA is issued to students - opening the entire Europe market for jobs and career-building.

After education the student is given a 1.5-year work VISA which will give him enough time to explore job and career opportunities PAN Europe. German laws are employee friendly, therefore, if a company dissolves government pays salaries. Job security and job satisfaction is very high in Germany as one need not work overtime. Mechanical and mechatronics are specializations for which Germany is the first choice. These days, the trend is that, graduates having a Computer background are opting for German Universities to pursue masters in AI or Data and Knowledge engineering as well as Machine Learning. Universities float nearly hundred or more subjects so that students can design their own curriculum by making a wise choice of courses and electives. Germany is a very safe country to live and the people here are friendly and willing to help. As the language of communication is German it is highly recommended to have German language proficiency. There have been instances where they do not respond to an English communication but definitely give you a response if the communication was made in German. A good resource for any help or support required is German Academic Exchange Service offices located in major cities. They may not counsel you which University to select but surely help with process guidance. These services are free of cost. The verdict is - pursuing higher education in Germany is highly recommended.

Higher Education in Ireland

The total cost of pursuing a Master's degree in Ireland is approximately 18 lakh INR, the breakup being 9-10 lakhs course fees and the remaining is for living expenses. The course duration is also shorter, at just 15 months as compared to 24 months course duration at other countries like USA and Germany. During VISA processing and University Application procedure, the proof of sponsors capability in the form of savings/FDs/Bank statements are to be submitted for verification. Unlike Germany you don't get a Schengen VISA. The rents are on the higher side as compared to Germany (400-500 Euros). As per Irish estimates you require around 10000 Euros per year as living expenses. If you are diligent and believe in saving, you may spend no more than 600 Euros per month. The curriculum is substantial as the course duration is less. The students have to be on their toes always to complete the academic requirements within timeline. English is a medium of communication and people are very friendly. The verdict is that, for people who cannot afford to pay the USA or UK fees and those who do not wish to go to Germany, Ireland can be a very good option due to the large saving promised in time and money!

Higher Education in USA

In order to obtain admission to a University in the USA, a student is required to apply for F1 student VISA costing around

200 dollars. Students aspiring to pursue MS in the USA has to appear for GRE exam, IELTS/TOEFL for English proficiency. The qualifying score for GRE should be above 310 to secure an admission in good colleges while the TOEFL score must be above 100. IELTS score is valid for all European Universities, TOEFL is specifically for USA. Preparation for GRE/TOEFL/ IELTS exams require undivided attention so it is recommended that candidates take this exam when they are not engaged in full time education or jobs or internships. The total exam fees are estimated at 14000 INR; GRE- 14000 INR, IELTS-14000 INR. A good IELTS score is above 7. The scores impact the college you may get admitted into, the internship or assistantship. Hence it is advised to carry out a thorough research of college, department and the course the student is trying to get admitted to. An average cost of 35-45 lakh INR per year, 19000 USD fee per semester, expenses to the tune of USD 1500 per month (800-900 dollars rent and rest monthly expenses) must be arranged for. Sponsors savings/FDs/Bank Statements/ Bank assurance letter/ Loan sanction letter will help in getting admission. Fall-August will offer more job opportunities than Spring-January. Coaching for exams cost 30000 INR approximately. Candidates may apply to colleges they aspire to join and are more or less confident of getting into. Application fees per candidate is around 5000 INR. From the job perspective, coding skills and problem solving skills are key determinants of success. For admission, following the SOP is very critical. It has to be unique and appealing. For VISA processing, the consultants usually charge around 10000 INR. The I20 document from University received at the college

mailing address is a major document for VISA sanction. The verdict is that, if you can afford you must aspire to acquire an MS in the USA as it is a very exceptional experience in terms of learning, professor expertise, and state-of-the-art labs. As the popular saying goes, 'USA is a land of opportunities'.

A good online resource which can be extremely useful for admission to foreign Universities, is the YOCKET portal.

All the numbers mentioned above are pre-pandemic derived from first hand sources for the year 2019. The course content delivery and fees may vary post-pandemic.

4

AFTER 10TH ALTERNATIVE CAREER OPTIONS

A call from a colleague, a friend or a relative seeking advice on what career path their ward must choose after taking up 10th Grade exams, has become commonplace for me. Parents usually want their children to join safer conventional courses and end up being either a doctor/engineer/civil servant/bank probationary officer or any similar government occupation. The millennials, on the other hand, want to fly aeroplanes, rockets, drones or do photography or be a cricketer or be a NASA scientist or participate in MasterChef to become a world class chef or aspire to be a movie actor. A lot of frustration can be sensed among parents in order to make a correct choice.

A simple remedy to this, is that if one is confused, he must go to a career counsellor and take professional help. Invest some money to get your ward appear for psychometric test. A psychometric test is a tool to help a student and his worried parents understand the former's likes and dislikes, skills and expertise levels which will help them make the right career choices.

The other angle to address the issue is that, as a parent, father, mother, brother, sister one has observed the student since his childhood so they are best judge of the ward's skillset. Keep an open eye, an astute ear, be inquisitive, ask questions to his subject teachers, class teachers and friends and voila! you know the answer to this million-dollar question.

By zeroing down on the student's interest area, one can get him admitted to a design school or hotel management program or pilot training or movie editing or acting school or many more alternative career options.

To quote Dr. Shirisha Sathe President R&D Shyamchi AAi foundation the days of Field are over and the days of individual have begun for career building. She says an individual has to be multiskilled. He has to prepare and upskill himself in such a way that he is ready to face transition every 3-5 years as the current field may saturate in that span of time. She further adds learning behaviour of the student matters the most and career choice is not an event but a process. The days of learning one skill and settling down are over because of rapid advancement in technology.

5

START-UP ECOSYSTEM

'I am a fresher, BE graduate. I don't want to do a routine 9-5 job. I don't like reporting to a boss. I don't like deadlines, timings, quarterly numbers. I want freedom. I will be an entrepreneur and join the start-up bandwagon.'

The above is a recipe for disaster. Be an entrepreneur and start a company if you are committed to the problem statement. It should personally affect you. You must be sure that the solution you are designing using technology has tremendous potential, it is scalable and is an innovative solution. As the founder of the company, you must understand that the primary responsibility rests on you for all decisions you take. The responsibility to be shouldered is 10 times more than the responsibility that an employee working in a company shoulders.

Before starting on your own, get some exposure by undertaking training and internship. Work, if possible, in a start-up; Work under bosses with varied exposure. Be flexible, stay late, gel well with the team where you are working.

Once you start your own company, your demeanour, body language and the way you carry yourself should be very professional. Your enthusiasm and positive energy should always be visible to your team. You must always appear upbeat. If you show low emotional intelligence, the entire start-up team gets affected. As your behaviour impacts everyone, always stay positive.

Build a Support system by surrounding yourself with people having varied experience. Update them about your activity and take inputs for course correction. Conduct mock sessions for investor pitch and client talk. Bring industry experts, brainstorm and improvise.

As regards contributors to success, I would believe that the share in percentage of idea versus execution is 20-25% Vs 75-80% respectively. For successful execution, processes must be put in place. They ought to be designed in such a way that even if the founders and key personnel are absent from the scene, the work should go on smoothly.

The journey of a start-up begins with a new product/service idea to proof of concept. From proof of concept to prototype and then product/idea refinement to commercial sale of the product/service.

The factor that differentiates a Start-up from any other business is scalability. The vision of the start-up should be grand. A relatable one-liner about your product vision should be ready. The product features, business model and revenue streams should be crystal clear, backed by numbers derived from extensive research. Scaling up or growing the differentiator is process orientation. Process orientation is the most monotonous part in the start-up journey yet the most important. Persistence should be the key quality of founders. The challenge lies in how well one deals with the mundane tasks which don't seem exciting. Starting a business sounds thrilling but running a business is gives you a reality check! Your excitement levels must never dim, and gather more zeal as time passes.

Iteration/pivoting/agility are key to success. If you find there are no takers for your product in the market, you might need to improvise on the model continuously and reposition yourself as per the market need.

Initial seed fund is to be raised by the founders themselves, with the help of their family and friends. After that an angel investor is to be scouted very carefully as he is the one who gradually he gets committed to your idea and the start-up journey itself. After that venture capitalists enter the scene. Each of the investors enters and exits by contributing effectively in the scaling of your company. Hence the core characteristic of your product should be innovative, technology assisted solutions, displaying exponential scalability and wealth creation capability. The investor journey ends with your company being publicly listed.

When pitching for funding you must realize that your investor is least interested in the profits your company is aspiring to earn. They are concerned about how fast it can scale so that they get a good exit and they earn good. An investor also expects your business model to be self-sustainable - meaning that it starts generating revenue from the very first year since the inception of the company.

Valuation of modern day tech/fintech start-ups does not use traditional methods like return on revenue. The valuation mechanism is intrinsic and depends on factors like scalability, wealth creation possibility and innovation.

Definition of a start-up as per Government of India (www.startupindia.gov.in) before 2017: inception to 5 years, revenue less than 25 crores and Innovation. After 2017: recognized by start-up India initiative, recognized by department of industrial policy and promotion, inception to 7 years, registered firm with Ministry of Corporate Affairs, turnover per year less than 25 crores for the 7 years; innovation, wealth creation and employment generation.

You can either register your company as a private limited company or as a limited liability partnership company. A Private

Limited Company looks more professional, and investors tend to take you more seriously but compliance required for commencement are more. Liability on the entrepreneur is relatively low. Taxation, however, is dual. It requires a minimum of 2 Directors. While forming a Limited Liability Company (LLC) is easier, Taxation processes are slow and also mandate a requirement of minimum 2 Directors.

To encourage young graduates, many start-up initiatives and schemes have been proposed by both by the Government and private entities. Every state in India has its own start-up initiative tied up with premier institutions like IITs. These institutions establish incubation centres. Few examples of States start-up Organisations are: www.msins.in, https://beabihar.in, https://hyderabad.tie.org/. An example of an Incubations centre at IITs is https://sineiitb.org/. The incubation centre conducts many events to attract young entrepreneurs. They even give seed fund to the tune of 10 Lakh, in addition to Incubation (mentoring, compliances, legal, technical) support.

An incubation centre provides the following: Support for business development, Initial growth funds, network and linkages, laboratory testing facilities, mentoring and advisory support. They also speedup the growth and success of your start-up. An incubation system is an ecosystem which guides the journey of your start-up, from idea to reality or from concept to product.

6

POST COVID 19 OPPORTUNITIES

I am writing this on 25-May-2020 and am a witness to the Corona catastrophe which is playing havoc all over the world. This mysterious virus by name Novel Corona Virus has humbled the strongest of the nations and mightiest of the leaders. Few say nature is doing course correction to man-made so called detrimental development in the form of concrete jungles and factories, and unwarranted pollution while a few state that it is an equalizer, as everybody will have to start afresh post the pandemic. Few also claim that we will have to learn to live with it while a few are optimistic that these tough times will pass.

What lessons should we lesser mortals - the middle class of India (be it a student or an employee, a woman or a man, a young or an adult) learn?

The takeaways are simple. We are going to face the biggest economic recession mankind has ever witnessed. We are not sure when will this pandemic end, when the vaccine will be available and how long will the economy take time to recover.

What we can do and what is within our means is to fight it with double the strength, triple the determination, ten-folds skill set acquisition, hundred folds' competitive spirit and a strong belief in oneself that we will sail through this safely. Few inputs:

Families should ensure that every member, is able to cook and do household chores. They should also ensure complete online work/learn/earn from home kit: separate laptop for each family member, good internet bandwidth, a room with good lighting, pleasing background so that your videos and meetings carry a good visual impact.

Every household, keeping the current dynamics in mind, must along with the current jobs and businesses explore multiple sources of income through frugal businesses - be it organic vegetables, online coaching or other essentials per se corona made requirements like masks and sanitizers.

The obsession of typical Indian working middle classes (getting a good job, buying a fancy car, purchasing a grand accommodation, big-fat weddings) should change to ensure that every household should be a cottage industry, self-sufficient and capable of producing start-ups and entrepreneurs. They must have acquired at least one life skill of designing, maintaining, repairing machines in daily use, in farms, in industries.

The foremost is slowly coming out of the houses, breathing fresh air, sunlight, walking and small careful outings to places where we used to frequent before the Corona outbreak.

Part – 2

5A's for Success and Growth

5A's for Success and Growth

Kevin Hall, Author "Aspire"

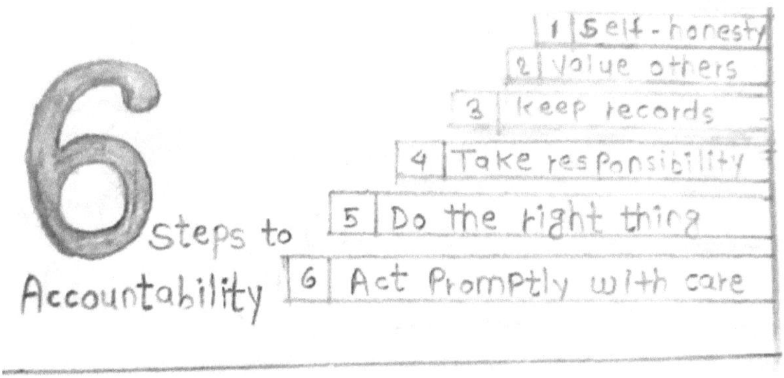

Eve Ash

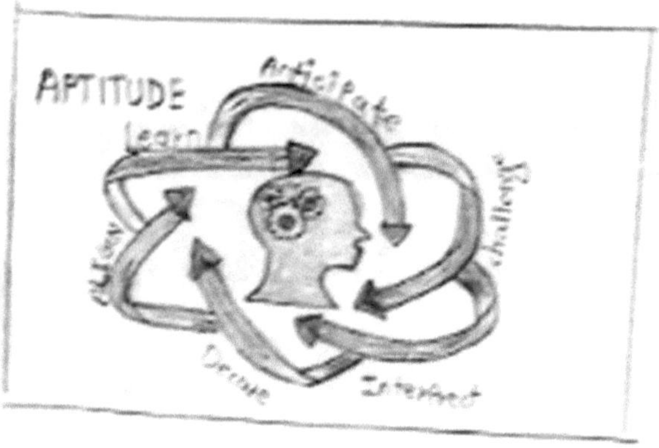

Source: http://www.eceway.com

Source: https://unfold1.wordpress.com/

7

PERSPECTIVE OF COMMUNICATION AND IMPORTANCE OF 5 A'S

I have grown up in a middle class family - my father was a Government servant and my mother, a home maker - but I am proud to say that it is because of their relentless effort that I am the person I am today.

In several ways, directly and remotely, they have been an inspiration during my whole journey till now, and I am sure will be till the very end.

During my growth years, all my learnings – at home and within my social circles-, have been very useful in my professional career and growth.

My father worked in 3 different states during his employment tenure, as his job had inherent transfer possibilities. Such mobility enabled him learn many languages, and he used to speak fluently around 10 languages. At one point, curiosity got the better of me and I asked him how he managed to learn all these languages.

He expressed that during his tenure at different locations, he used to work with local employees, labourers, contractors, and several others of their kind who only used to understand the local language. Thus, in order to gel with them and to get the work done effectively he realized that, talking to them in their own language, made it easier to boost their confidence, get the work done efficiently and avoid the possibility of any miscommunication. This strong logic paved way for his multi-lingual proficiency.

The importance of communication could never be belittled, and that's how I realized how important it is to communicate in a language that is comfortable to the person whom we are interacting with, so that they understand it right. Hence, trying to put yourself in the receivers shoes before sending any communication, helps you understand their issues in an improved manner, and might help you address their problem in a better way.

My father believed that one must be treated with respect, irrespective of the position they held. He never failed to respect the colleagues he interacted with, be it a labourer, a janitor, an office attendant, housekeeping staff, his peers or his superiors and subordinates. This has, in turn, helped him earn the respect from all the people he interacted. This was a great learning for me, and that is how I have learnt the significance of earning respect –through the conscious practice of give respect and earn respect - and I have tried to follow the same concept in my life.

After my graduation, I moved to Mumbai to join my first job and started staying with some acquaintances whom I met during the first job, and who soon went on to become my friends and room-mates. I slowly began to understand the role each of us had to play in that shared accommodation, and we subconsciously adorned roles of family members – sharing and caring for each other – and during that process when I was still a bachelor, learnt an eminent lesson that communication with each member in the house is quite essential, to sort out a lot of confusions and create a better bond between the members. I have stayed for around 7 years with my room-mates, but don't remember any incident where we ended up in a fight.

These principles, I have advocated and used earnestly during my professional tenure - communicate more, give respect to each individual irrespective of his level, keep things transparent, and apologize if you commit a mistake. A great bonding between colleagues may be created by a culture that nurtures transparency and openness.

Now let me explain why I feel that these 5A's are the most important ones in any person's life; and I am sure it will help you both personally and professionally.

During my journey thus far I realized that whether you are studying or employed, technical expertise, domain knowledge, operational knowledge, processes, etc. can be acquired, but if individuals still face problem with these 5A's (Attitude, Aspiration, Aptitude, Accountability and Arrogance) and if the ratio between the A's is not appropriate; even the best knowledge & technical expertise, cannot come to his rescue, and he is bound to fail in his career. I have seen many of my juniors, peers as well as seniors failing because of lack of the correct proportion of these 5A's.

As in Industries/companies, you have to work with different types of people, different roles, different levels, different capabilities and different skills; in order to succeed you have to work with all such individual in a team with singular focus on the organization goal. In such a scenario if an individual, in spite of having all the knowledge and expertise, is not able to work well with or gel with the team because of the lack of any of this 5A's; it is a failure for the individual, the team and the organization. This is the reason why I feel that these are the most important 5A's for any individual, for growth and success.

8

THE 1ST A – ATTITUDE

Kevin Hall, Author "Aspire"

"As per definition, it is "a settled way of thinking or feeling about something." (as per the online Dictionary www.dictionary.com)

It's the point of view, the way of thinking.

According to Maio and Olson, "The attitude of a person is determined by psychological factors like ideas, values, beliefs, perception, etc. All these have a complex role in determining a person's attitude. Values are ideals, guiding principles in one's life, or overarching goals that people strive to obtain."

This means that attitude is based on your growth stages, from child to teenager and then to an adult. During this process, whatever you have experienced or you have observed around you helps you build that attitude with the right frame of mind.

I personally feel it is the most important factor in any person. If you have the right attitude, there is no limit to growth - it will help to create positivity around.

However, the corollary is that, if you have the wrong attitude, it will destroy relationships, malign the environment, and create lot of negativity around you.

Thus the person with right attitude, keeps himself grounded, understands the problems while addressing alternatives, ensures that it is not adversely impacting stakeholders, and sees the bigger picture for organizational advantage, rather than just take decisions for his personal growth and benefit.

I have found that people with right attitude are always good team players and will be key players in the team and organizational growth if right motivation is provided. Further such people are mostly ethical and ready to grow on the path provided.

Similarly, people with wrong attitude work for their personal benefit, adjudged bad team players, and chances are bright that they might subordinate organizational interest to achieve their personal goals. Such people tend to follow unethical practices to achieve their self-centred goals.

Zig Zagler "See You at The Top"

In my journey so far, I have seen many team members and seniors with right attitude, doing great things and creating a culture of mutual growth. Similarly, I have also noticed a lot of people engaged in misdeeds, with the objective of growing personally for their own little benefits.

So nowadays, getting colleagues with the right attitude at all levels - campus hires to the executive level - is the key for any organization to grow.

I personally feel that when you are chosen for a role at senior level, it is largely because of your experience and knowledge. Hence it is your moral and professional duty to guide the juniors when they make mistakes. If your attitude is right only then will you be able to do that, else, many at times it gets into a shade of bossism, and sends the wrong message to the entire organization, who will have problems working with your attitude issues.

9

THE 2ND A – ASPIRATION

As per definition, it is "a hope or ambition of achieving something." (as per the online Dictionary www.dictionary.com)

Everyone should have some aspiration in life, else there is no sense of purpose to one's living.

Aspiration could be interpreted as a personal goal to achieve and it helps to keep you intrinsically motivated.

Source: https://thriveglobal.com/stories/the-stairs-to-success/

The level of aspirations depends on your background, upbringing, learning environment, etc. Every person tends to have different aspirations and the level of aspirations per person also keeps on changing as you start achieving them.

A candid reference can be made to Maslow's Hierarchy of needs here. People, who are from very poor economic backgrounds, may have a base aspiration to own a small 1 room independent house, but once they achieve it they may think of a bigger house or a vehicle, which is a higher order need.

Similarly, a person from a rich background already has the basic needs and more, so his level of aspirations may be at a much higher level than that we saw in the earlier example.

A person who might be at an entry level job might aspire to reach the topmost position some day and begin working towards it from the very start.

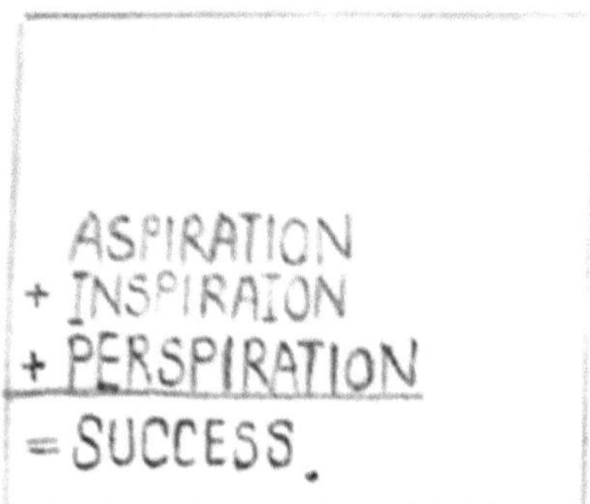

Source: http://thingsweforget.blogspot.com

So in short, every person poor or rich, educated or uneducated always has an aspiration, so when we hire people it becomes extremely important for the organization to understand the aspirations of such candidates, as often times if the aspirations are aligned to the organizational growth properly, it can work wonders.

On the other hand, if it is not done appropriately, it can damage the whole equation and adversely impact the organization.

10

THE 3RD A – APTITUDE

As per definition, it is "a natural ability to do something." (as per the online Dictionary www.dictionary.com)

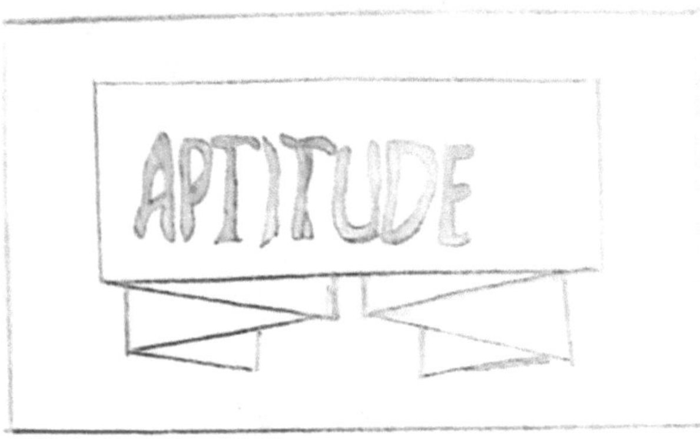

Every person has a different aptitude, and that is a primary reason why most of the organizations take aptitude tests during the screening of candidates for hire. The belief underlying the process is that, a person having a good aptitude for a role can be taught new things and he would grasp it quickly. Hence, catching up with the latest technologies, cross-skilling, upgrading - all becomes easy.

If aptitude is low, it is always a challenge for the employee and also for the organization to grow, since such person will always be on the lookout for excuses why he should NOT do things.

Even at the senior level, I have found that people with less aptitude are more negative in their approach, while people with good aptitude are positively inclined.

With people who take time to understand things and find ways to avoid work, it is futile to expect that they will turnaround things.

Change is the only constant, and is so much part of our daily lives - at every level, every new role, every new company - and if our aptitude is good, we try to find out ways to understand the change and get it implemented, and also imbibe the change from within which helps in growth.

Aptitude has a big role to play in faster learning, aptly anticipating, better interpreting, taking right decisions, getting easily aligned to the organizational mission and managing challenges very well.

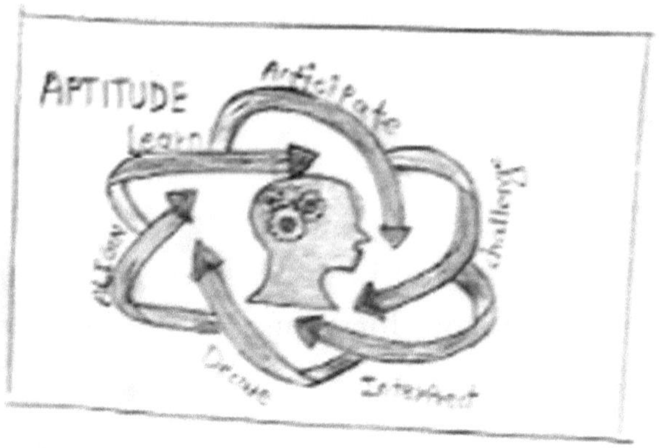

Source: http://www.eceway.com

Based on my experience, I sense that people with good aptitude are also superior in all above tasks and this is one of the reasons why they are on a fast track growth path and become excellent leaders.

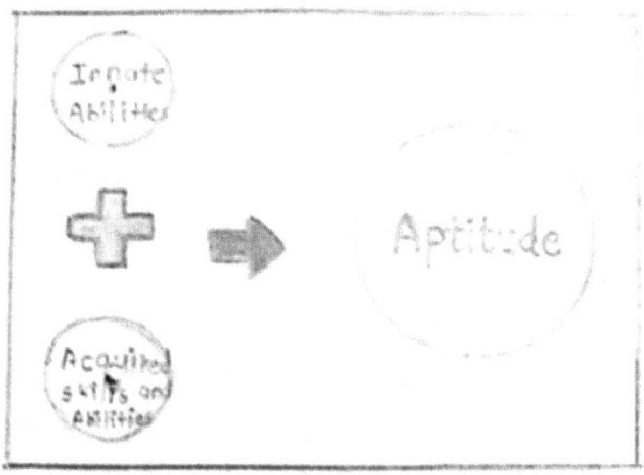

11

THE 4TH A – ACCOUNTABILITY

As per definition, it is "the fact or condition of being accountable; responsibility." (as per the online Dictionary www.dictionary.com)

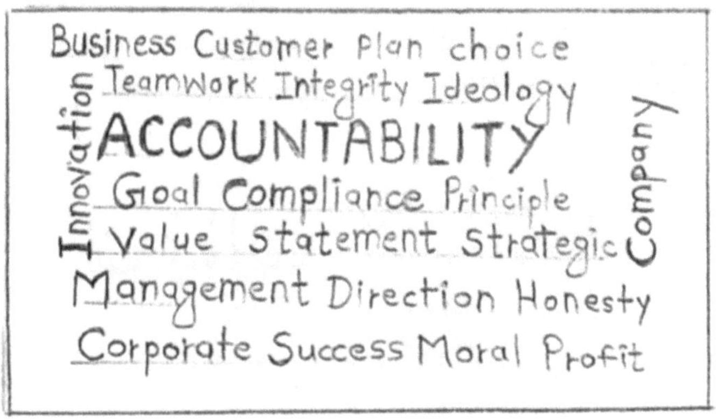

Source: https://www.canstockphoto.com

This is also one of the key factors underpinning success rate in a career. A person who is accountable is always ready to take up the work responsibilities with ownership and keenly focused on the achievement of results. Such individuals are self-motivated, often define their own goals and ensure that they achieve it, without having superiors reminding them or pursuing them constantly.

As a student also, several of my friends who were very good in studies and excel, were not in a competition with anyone but themselves. It was more about getting all answers correct, which was the focus and the driving factor. As such most of them were the toppers in their batch and gold medallists; who later on excelled in their career. They all were accountable to themselves and had set their own goals.

In the same way when we are working, it is the responsibility and accountability that gives each individual success; it helps you keep yourself motivated and grow incessantly.

Bob proctor

In my experience, any individual who works with accountability is on the growth path and will continue to grow. During interviews we do look for people with such skills for leadership roles, since selecting a person with poor accountability traits, will always end up in situations where they tend to trouble their peers. They will be found spending more time proving how it was another's mistake, and this is definitely not a good practice. People who are accountable are always committed to provide results.

As an individual, an accountable person follows the below 6 elements s which helps in the growth of the individual, his team as well as his organization.

The important 6 steps are

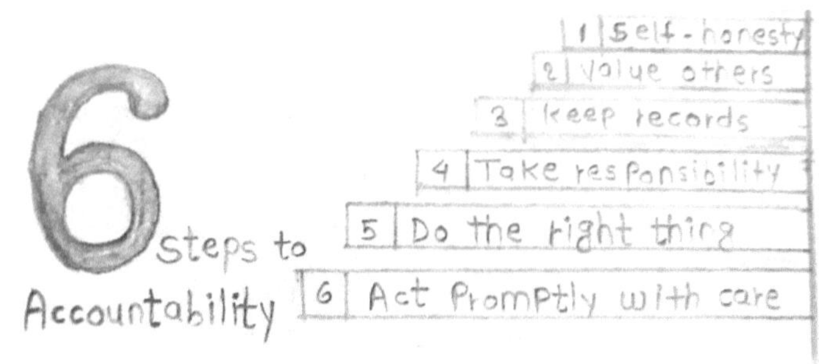

Eve Ash

12

THE 5TH A – ARROGANCE

As per definition, it is "the quality of being arrogant." (as per the online Dictionary www.dictionary.com)

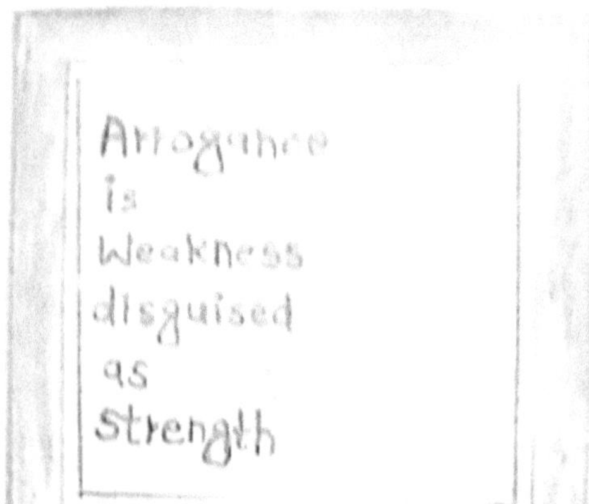

Source: https://boldomatic.com

An arrogant person only feels smart if someone else feels stupid. Their sense of themselves depends on thinking less of someone else. They insist on correcting other people's grammar or showing them their flaws, as it seems the only way they can feel an approximation of confidence. Arrogance is about intent: it is when ability (or perceived ability) is used to look down on others.

If arrogance is present in a person, after acquiring a lot of experience and knowledge, it is acceptable to a limit. It can be compared to salt in a dish! Though we agree that salt is indispensable for taste in the food, it has to be in the right ratio, only then does it improve the dish, else it can be ruined. Arrogance likewise, in appropriate proportions may help you as a leader.

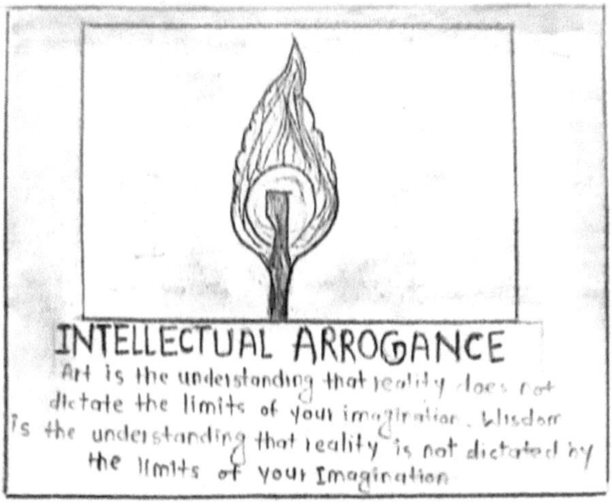

Source: https://www.pinterest.com

Excess salt in the best food you prepare, will make it impossible for you to eat.

In the same way if arrogance is more, then you will tend to have problems with such person.

With the trend visible in the current demographics - where every family is nuclear in nature with a single kid - you can see lot of teenagers and millennial adults with ostensible arrogance. They don't seem to have the knowledge or expertise, but still appear highly arrogant and completely dismiss the idea of listening to or following instructions of anyone.

In the industry also if you have colleagues who are arrogant, then they seem to clearly lack good team player skills and you have challenges getting work done with them in a team.

If the leader is arrogant, then you can see challenges in him managing his team, which may result in more attrition in his team.

Confidence and arrogance are 2 different things.

A confident person feels competent from the inside out. They use their talents to genuinely try to be of use, or to succeed at the task at hand. They might seek external validation, but they don't depend on it to define their sense of their ability or nature.

In some cases, an arrogant person may have more skill than a confident person, but confident people will tend to wield the abilities they have with more composure and command than an arrogant person.

Author's Note to Readers

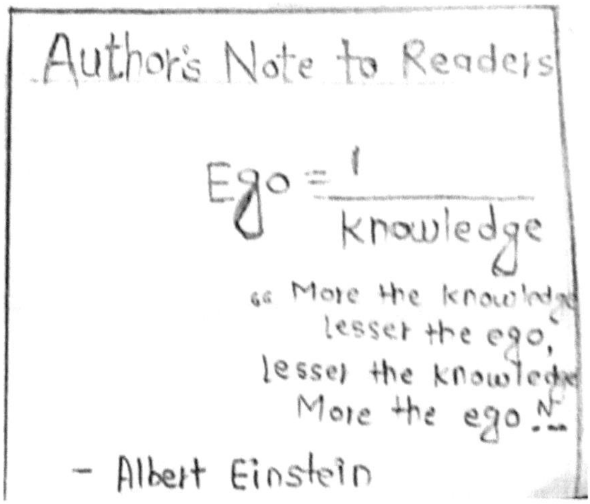

Hope you might have realized while reading Part 2 of the book, as to how the 5A's indirectly help in the growth of individuals and also how it might, in the long run, adversely impact the growth if you ignore them. So it is always better to have a self-realization and be grounded, no matter what level you reach; so that you respect others, value others and in turn earn respect and immense satisfaction.

– Sumesh Menon

Gratitude

Thanks a lot for your valuable time extended for reading this book, and we genuinely hope we were able to provide some value-add to you. If you have any suggestions please feel free to reach out to us on umapublicationsned@gmail.com, so that it will help us to refine our next book.

– Rajesh Kulkarni

– Sumesh Menon

www.ingramcontent.com/pod-product-compliance
Lightning Source LLC
Chambersburg PA
CBHW050025170726
48282CB00025B/551